THANK YOU,
Mom

WRITTEN BY M.H. CLARK

DESIGNED BY JESSICA PHOENIX

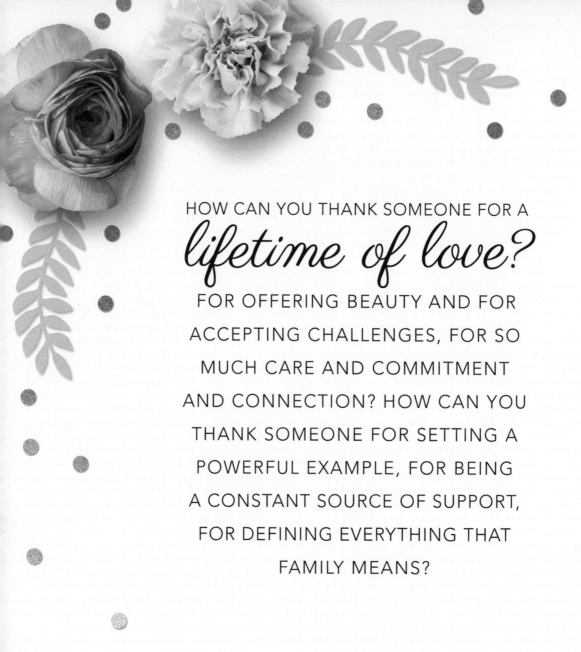

HOW CAN YOU THANK SOMEONE FOR A

lifetime of love?

FOR OFFERING BEAUTY AND FOR ACCEPTING CHALLENGES, FOR SO MUCH CARE AND COMMITMENT AND CONNECTION? HOW CAN YOU THANK SOMEONE FOR SETTING A POWERFUL EXAMPLE, FOR BEING A CONSTANT SOURCE OF SUPPORT, FOR DEFINING EVERYTHING THAT FAMILY MEANS?

Mom, THERE IS SO MUCH TO THANK YOU FOR. THERE ARE SO MANY YEARS OF LOVE AND WORK THAT IT'S HARD TO KNOW WHERE TO BEGIN. SO ALL I CAN DO IS SAY IT SIMPLY, WITH GREAT HEART AND GREAT SINCERITY: *thank you.* FOR ALL THAT YOU HAVE BEEN AND ALL THAT YOU ARE. IT MATTERS EVEN MORE THAN YOU KNOW.

WITH LOVE,

_____

ALL THAT IS WORTH
CHERISHING BEGINS
IN THE HEART...

Suzanne Chapin

THANK YOU,
MOM,
FOR *days* TO
remember.

...SHE WAS THE SAME
INSIDE AS I AM...

Anna Swir

I'M SO
grateful
FOR
everything
WE SHARE.

*How strange,
exciting and miraculous
that we can change each
other so much, love each
other so much...*

LAURIE ANDERSON

I APPRECIATE OUR
connection.

LOVE IS NOT SOMETHING
WE GIVE OR GET; IT IS
SOMETHING THAT WE
NURTURE AND GROW...

Brené Brown

Thanks
for growing
with me.

You are a part

of all that I am.

THOSE WHO LIVE PASSIONATELY
TEACH US HOW TO LOVE.
THOSE WHO LOVE PASSIONATELY
TEACH US HOW TO LIVE.

Sarah Ban Breathnach

THANK YOU, MOM,
FOR YOUR
example.

The love
WE GIVE AWAY IS THE
only love
WE KEEP.

Elbert Hubbard

I'M SO GRATEFUL FOR
your generous heart.

WE'LL DO IT TOGETHER.

Molly Fumia

I appreciate your being there.

Very little
IS NEEDED TO MAKE A
happy life...

MARCUS AURELIUS

Thanks

FOR EACH EVERYDAY GIFT.

YOU MAKE
shared
moments
COUNT.

A GOOD PERSON IS A
GIFT TO THE WHOLE WORLD.

Heidi Wills

THANK YOU,
Mom,
FOR KNOWING HOW
TO MAKE THINGS
better.

EVERYTHING IS HELD
TOGETHER WITH STORIES.

Barry Lopez

I'm so grateful for our history.

MAYBE HAPPINESS DIDN'T
HAVE TO BE ABOUT THE BIG,
SWEEPING CIRCUMSTANCES,
ABOUT HAVING EVERYTHING
IN YOUR LIFE IN PLACE. MAYBE
IT WAS ABOUT STRINGING
TOGETHER A BUNCH OF
SMALL PLEASURES.

Ann Brashares

I APPRECIATE
*every single
special day.*

ONE GESTURE. ONE PERSON.
ONE MOMENT AT A TIME.

Libba Bray

THANKS FOR MAKING
MY LIFE MORE
beautiful.

You shape
my world for
the better.

LIKE ALL
magnificent things,
IT'S VERY SIMPLE.

Natalie Babbitt

Thank you, Mom,
FOR SHOWING ME THE WAY.

LIFE IS WHAT YOU
CELEBRATE. ALL OF IT.

Joanne Harris

I'M SO
grateful
FOR THE
years we've
shared.

...YOU ARE
*beautiful
already.*

VICTORIA MORAN

I APPRECIATE YOUR
incredible spark.

To me, you will be unique in all the world. To you, I shall be unique in all the world.

ANTOINE DE SAINT-EXUPÉRY

Thanks

FOR YOUR RARE SPIRIT.

You live and love

with all your heart.

I AM STILL LEARNING.

Michelangelo

THANK YOU,
Mom,
FOR YOUR
patience.

SOMETIMES
words
ARE NOT ENOUGH.

Lemony Snicket

I'M SO GRATEFUL FOR ALL THE WAYS *you love me.*

YOU AND I ARE MORE
THAN YOU AND I...

e e cummings

I appreciate everything we've become.

...LIFE GROWS LOVELY
WHERE YOU ARE...

Mathilde Blind

THANKS FOR ADDING

so much

beauty

TO MY LIFE.

You are my
past, my present,
and my future.

MOTHER IS A VERB.
IT'S SOMETHING YOU DO.
NOT JUST WHO YOU ARE.

Cheryl Lacey Donovan

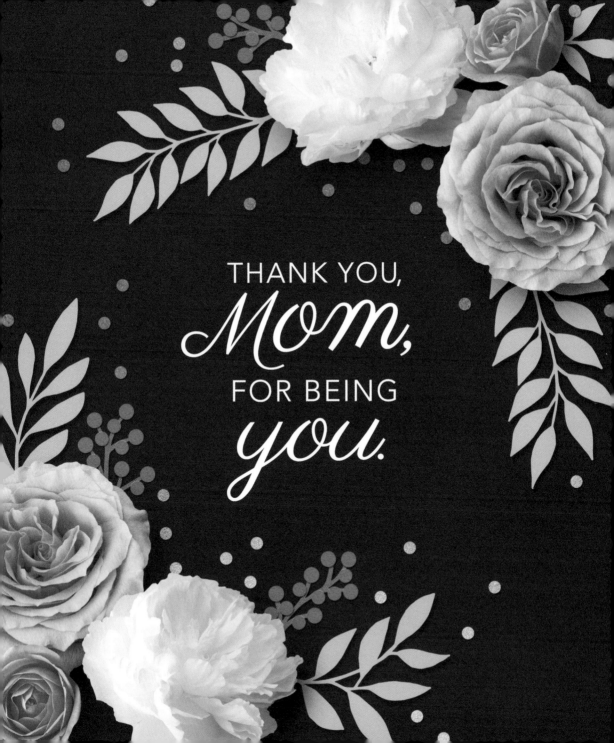

THANK YOU,
Mom,
FOR BEING
you.

COMPENDIUM.

live inspired

With special thanks to the entire Compendium family.

Credits:
WRITTEN & COMPILED BY: M.H. CLARK
DESIGNED BY: JESSICA PHOENIX
EDITED BY: AMELIA RIEDLER

ISBN: 978-1-938298-82-0

3RD PRINTING. PRINTED IN CHINA WITH SOY INKS.